IT'S MOVE

OUT LOUD

TWELVE INTERACTIVE GAME-BASED
SMALL GROUP SESSIONS

TOM ELLSWORTH

Standard®
PUBLISHING
Cincinnati, Ohio

Published by Standard Publishing, Cincinnati, Ohio

www.standardpub.com

Copyright © 2010 by Tom Ellsworth

Printed in: USA

Cover design: DesignWorks

Interior design: Dorcas Design & Typesetting

ISBN 978-0-7847-2362-3

15 14 13 12 11 10   1 2 3 4 5 6 7 8 9

CONTENTS

HOW TO PLAY THIS BOOK

The It's Your Move small group series was designed to get your group playing, interacting, talking, and connecting together through the study of God's Word and will for your lives. Here are some gaming tips on how to get the most out of this experience.

Each topic is divided into two parts: **GAME ON** and **POSTGAME BREAKDOWN**. These sessions were conceived as happening in two separate, consecutive small group meetings. However, you may of course choose to use them in whatever way works best for your group.

In **GAME ON**, group members play a lively game together and talk briefly about the themes presented in that particular game. The six games used throughout the book are classics that have been around for some time, thus it is likely that the members of your group or other people you know will have a copy (or copies) that you will be able to borrow for use in your small group meeting. Depending on how much time and how many players you have available, you may choose to play one entire game, hold a tournament, or use one of the abbreviated versions of the game that has been suggested. If your group has members with children who also attend the small group meetings, it's easy to include them in the fun. We have offered suggestions for how to do that for each game session.

Further discussion on the game's themes and what the Bible has to say about these issues is carried on in the second session—**POSTGAME BREAKDOWN**. You will be given a Bible passage to study along with questions and commentary that help you dig deep into the meaning of God's Word. As you work through these studies, be sure to allow each person to have a chance to take part in making connections—this part is not a competition! Allow everyone an opportunity to voice their opinions.

Throughout the book, you will notice two kinds of questions, which we've titled **Take Turns** and **Your Spin**. The **Take Turns** questions are meant for group conversation, while the **Your Spin** questions are intended for personal exploration, though you may choose to share those answers with your fellow members as you wish. At the end of each of the postgame sessions you will find practical ideas for your group to take action and make your move by reaching out to your world in tangible ways. This could even develop into a third session for your group, a time when you meet to work and serve others together.

We hope you and your group enjoy these twelve interactive sessions. There's a lot here for you to experience as you build your relationships with God and each other. What are you waiting for? It's your move.

CRANIUM:

Seeking Common Sense in a Confusing World

PART ONE—GAME ON

Object of the Game

Are you right-brained? Or maybe left? Either way the CRANIUM game will give you the chance to shine where you are gifted—and struggle where you aren't. But the point is to use what you know to make sense of the game.

Game Preparation

The CRANIUM game is designed to be played with four individuals or four groups. Decide which route you will take as that will determine how many game sets you will need. If you choose individual play, you will need one playing surface and game set for every four players. If you choose four teams, then one game should be sufficient. Team seating can be flexible to accommodate your space. Depending on how animated your players are, you may need some room for people to move around.

> "One pound of learning requires ten pounds of common sense to apply it."
>
> —Persian proverb

Use the four basic game colors—red, blue, yellow, and green—to decorate for your Game On session. You can scatter about pictures or sketches of the brain to add a touch of intellect (avoid any image reminiscent of Dr. Frankenstein's use of the brain—not the look you're going for).

Using markers and poster board, create examples of mathematical equations and fun word puzzles. Add a few posters of entertainers and artists to highlight the variety of talents represented in the game.

Playing by the Rules

The CRANIUM game is all about involving everyone and discovering and/or enjoying your talents. There are four categories for point-earning responses:

- Data Head—Here is your opportunity to demonstrate your ability to answer tough questions. You walking computers out there can put your mental hard drive to work and reveal your superior command of knowledge.

- Creative Cat—Are you gifted with artsy flair? This is your lucky break to draw or sculpt your way to victory.

- Word Worm—Perhaps you are one of those people who never goes anywhere without having on hand a crossword puzzle or sudoku book. This category was made for your deciphering genius.

- Star Performer—For you American Idol show wannabes, here is where you light up the room with song, dance, or drama.

There are various versions of the game available. If you are looking for a slightly different version of the original, you might try:

- CRANIUM: THE FAMILY FUN GAME—similar to the original, with minor changes.

- CRANIUM WOW—includes new cards and activities.

- CRANIUM KABOOKI—a video version available on the Wii platform.

If time is an issue, consider using one of the following:

- CRANIUM TURBO EDITION—a faster version.

- CRANIUM HOOPLA—takes only twenty minutes to play.

TRIVIA

What do you do after you've been named "employee of the year" at Microsoft? Three years later you quit and create a new, award-winning board game. At least, that's what Richard Tait did in 1997. After a rainy weekend of playing games with friends in the Hamptons, Tait decided to create a game where all players got a chance to highlight their talents. He convinced coworker Whit Alexander to leave Microsoft and join him in the adventure. Friends thought they had lost their minds. Quite the opposite was true—they gave people a real chance to use their brains like never before. Just imagine what you can do if you really crank up the ol' cranium!

If you are playing teams, have each team member participate in every activity:

- Data Head—all must confer on the response before answering.

- Star Performer—all must sing, dance, or perform together.

- Creative Cat—all must help sculpt or draw, regardless of the talent level.

- Word Worm—all must work together to solve the puzzle.

To Eat

The brain is a picky eater, preferring carbohydrates over any other food group. A few carbs (even the brain knows moderation is best) can be really soothing, like relaxing music for the mind. The best brain foods are fish and eggs. So here are some treat ideas for your gathering:

- Fresh fruit—for the carbs!

- Deviled eggs (or angeled eggs if you prefer), cups of custard, or individual soufflés (see recipe that follows).

- Fish sticks, fish tacos, salmon patties, tuna fish sandwiches, etc. Have something from the sea just for the halibut! (Sorry!)

- Goldfish-shaped crackers—yes, I know there is no real fish value here but hey, they're tasty.

If the brain food idea doesn't whet your appetite, you might try right-brained/left-brained snacks. Divide the snack table into two sections. Set one side with hearty but plain snacks: slices of cheese, beef log, apples, pretzels, etc. On the other side use unique and artistically decorated snacks: vegetable tray with delicately carved veggies, cupcakes or muffins with creative toppings, bread bowls with clam chowder, etc. Get creative. After all, that's part of the game!

For Younger Players

If you choose to go the team route, then the kids can easily be incorporated as part of the teams. If not, look for the kid's edition of the CRANIUM game called CADOO. This junior version of the game contains some elements of the familiar, kid-friendly tic-tac-toe. If, however, you have only one or two children who don't want to participate as team members, you can still involve them in the excitement. Give them official titles and jobs:

- Mr. Sandman (or Miss Sandwoman)—turns the sand-filled timer and watches until the glass runs empty. If you have a whistle or buzzer that the Sandman can use to signal the end of the turn, it will enhance the job.

3 TABLESPOONS BUTTER

3 TABLESPOONS ALL-PURPOSE FLOUR

¼ TEASPOON GROUND MUSTARD

DASH OF CAYENNE PEPPER

1 CUP MILK

1 CUP SHREDDED CHEDDAR, SWISS OR OTHER FAVORITE CHEESE

4 EGG WHITES

4 EGG YOLKS

Grease four 10-oz. soufflé dishes and set them on a baking sheet. Preheat oven to 350 degrees F. Beat room-temperature egg whites in a clean mixing bowl until stiff peaks form. Set aside. Melt the butter in a small saucepan. Whisk in the flour, mustard, and pepper until smooth; then slowly add the milk to the mixture. Bring just to a boil; cook for 1 to 2 minutes or until thickened, stirring constantly. Reduce heat to low; stir in cheese until melted. Remove pan from the heat. Stir a small amount of the butter, milk, and cheese mixture into the yolks; then gradually add the yolks to the pan, stirring constantly. Cool the mixture slightly. Once the pan mixture has cooled, fold the egg whites gently into it. Pour the batter into the greased dishes or cups. Bake for 20 minutes in the middle of the oven or until a knife inserted near the center comes out clean. Serve immediately. (You can double the recipe for more people or use smaller-size cups for bite-size soufflés. Muffin cups can work if they have straight sides. You will need to adjust the baking time. The finished soufflés should be a golden brown color and puffed up.)

- Princess Diecast (or Prince)—the official caster of the multicolored die at the end of play, which determines how far the game piece is moved.
- Claymaker—keeps the sculpting clay ready to use. After each use, Claymaker molds it back into a simple ball and readies it for the next turn.

As you play the game together, talk about how different kinds of knowledge and understanding help people work out problems. Take opportunities to point out to the kids the way God has blessed each person with a brain that works in different ways and how we need each other to make sense of the world together.

Picking Up the Pieces

After an entertaining cranial pursuit, consider how many talents were represented by everyone in your group. How did these talents help people deal with their struggles? What kinds of brain power seemed to work best?

Want to grow in common sense? Starting tomorrow, read one whole chapter of Proverbs each day for a month full of wise counsel. Close by praying for one another that God will bless each with:

- knowledge of God.

- understanding of God's truth.

- wisdom from God's Word.

TAKE TURNS

1. As time goes by, does life seem more confusing to you, or less? What kinds of things make our lives so perplexing?

2. How do each person's strengths or weaknesses make a difference to how they play this game? Do you notice any category having an advantage over others? If so, how?

3. How would you define common sense? How does it differ from other kinds of knowledge?

CRANIUM:
Seeking Common Sense in a Confusing World

Object of the Study

Use the brain that God gave you. Discover the truth. Be wise in a crowd of fools; be an island of sense in a sea of stupidity. Seek common sense in a confusing world.

Bible Content

Jesus, the master communicator, used a distinctive parable to draw a contrast between the wise and the foolish. Read the two versions of that story:

> Therefore everyone who hears these words of mine and puts them into practice is like a wise man who built his house on the rock. The rain came down, the streams rose, and the winds blew and beat against that house; yet it did not fall, because it had its foundation on the rock. But everyone who hears these words of mine and does not put them into practice is like a foolish man who built his house on sand. The rain came down, the streams rose, and the winds blew and beat against that house, and it fell with a great crash.
>
> —Matthew 7:24-27

> Why do you call me, "Lord, Lord," and do not do what I say? I will show you what he is like who comes to me and hears my words and puts them into practice. He is like a man building a house, who dug down deep and laid the foundation on rock. When a flood came, the torrent struck that house but could not shake it, because it was well built. But the one who hears my words and does not put them into practice is like a man who built a house on the ground without a foundation. The moment the torrent struck that house, it collapsed and its destruction was complete.
>
> —Luke 6:46-49

To Study

Perhaps I'm wrong, but it seems to me that some aspects of our culture can be confusingly foolish:

- In some cities a pizza will arrive at your door faster than an ambulance.

- Is your new, high-priced car unprotected in the driveway while your junk is protected in the garage?

- Have you ever driven several miles out of your way to save money on gas?

And we can be just as confusing with our words:

- "It's the same difference." Really?

- Why is going uptown or downtown always the same direction?

- Have you noticed that a "fat chance" is no better than a "slim chance"?

What about our confusing philosophies?

- "There is no absolute truth." Isn't that an absolute statement?

- "All truth is relative." Is that statement relative, too?

- "Everyone is on a different path going to the same place." Who came up with that one?

With so much confusion in actions, words, and philosophies, it's no wonder people struggle to make sense of it all.

TAKE TURNS

1. Read "Searching for the true foundation." What's your reaction when someone offers you personal experience, logical conclusions, or practical relevance as a basis for truth?

2. How would you respond to the statement "There is no absolute truth?"

3. Is there more than one spiritual path to Heaven? How do you know if you are traveling on the right one?

1. On a scale of 1 to 10, with 10 being the most, how would you rate your reliance on common sense in daily life?

2. What things about your world right now are most confusing to you? How do you make sense of these things? How does your faith in God help you?

3. What do you find most difficult about relating to people with other sources of truth?

Things are not always what they seem to be. Take this little quiz (answers at the end of this chapter).

1. How long did the Hundred Years' War last?
2. Which country makes Panama hats?
3. From what animal do we get catgut?
4. What is a camel's hairbrush made of?
5. The Canary Islands in the Pacific are named after what animal?
6. What was the first name of King George VI?
7. What color is a purple finch?
8. Where do Chinese gooseberries come from?

SEARCHING FOR THE TRUE FOUNDATION

The search for sense in our world happens on a continual basis—at least as often as people start building homes. In Luke's version of the parable Jesus told, we read that the first man building a house "dug down deep and laid the foundation on rock." How deep do we usually dig to search for a foundation for our beliefs?

Consider the sources where many go. Personal experience is one. Experience has become a primary source of truth for many. People who depend on this source might say "This must be true because of what I saw/heard/touched/sensed inside my heart." Approaching truth so subjectively is seldom, if ever, reliable.

Others depend on making logical conclusions. Logic alone determines truth. Through means of deduction or successfully repeated scenarios, the results are deemed true. Though often accurate, a purely logical approach is not foolproof. Even Sherlock Holmes's deductive genius didn't always lead him to the truth and his literary creator knew the end of the story!

Still others depend on practical relevance to find out truth for themselves: "The only relevant truth for my life is whatever works for me." Therefore, truth is not only pragmatic, but relative. And truth is personal; the same truth doesn't work for everyone, but no one has the right to claim his truth is superior.

So which created truth is right? Therein lies the problem—truth isn't created, it is revealed.

A preacher friend of mine, Dan Lang, wrote, "The uniqueness of Christianity is rooted in Jesus himself. When all other religious leaders say, 'I'll show you how to find truth,' Jesus says, 'I am truth.' They say, 'I'll show you the way to be enlightened.' Jesus says, 'I am the Light of the world.' They say, 'I'll show you the doors that lead to God.' Jesus declares, 'I am the door. I am the way'" (from a sermon given at Western Hills Church of Christ, Cincinnati, Ohio).

Submitting to the true foundation

In Luke 6 we read that Jesus started off his story with this question: "Why do you call me, 'Lord, Lord,' and do not do what I say?" It's a legitimate question, isn't it?

TAKE TURNS

1. Why are we so repelled by the word submit?

2. Is submission to God's truth something you find difficult to swallow? Why is that?

3. What are some reasons people are so reluctant to accept the truth of God? Why is the true story of Jesus so polarizing?

We go to Jesus with our problems and our complaints, asking "Please, Lord" will you do this or that—but do we then actually let him be Lord of our everyday lives?

Consider the sense of this story. When our first daughter was born she, like many babies, developed a bit of jaundice—a common liver disorder, which produces a yellowish skin cast. Untreated, it can be devastating, but a cure was simple. Babies then were kept under a special light; the body absorbed the light, which stimulated liver function.

Suppose when the doctor informed me about her condition, I became indignant: "This is *my* daughter; don't tell me how to take care of her. I can handle this on my own, thank you—I don't need your answers." Or if in denial I said, "She doesn't look yellow to me. Are you sure she's sick?" I could have postulated, "In fairness to the medical community, I should consult with our dentist and veterinarian before treatment." I could have questioned the physician's prescribed cure: "You mean to tell me that exposure to light is going to solve this? Nothing could be that simple." Innovatively, I might have offered, "Bleach takes color out—I think I'll just give her a bleach bath."

What would the doctor have said? "You don't understand, Tom. There is only one way to cure jaundice—just one way. Trust me; she has to be exposed to the light."

Regardless of the sincerity of my feelings, experience, logic, or pragmatism, all my efforts would have been futile. Submitting to the truth was the only hope.

The truth is, every one of us has a devastating illness that has darkened our lives. But the cure is simple—trust me, we must be exposed to the Light!

> "A handful of common sense is worth a bushel of learning."
> —Anonymous

BUILDING ON THE TRUE FOUNDATION

Once you've discovered the true foundation, you can build a true life. In the story of the two builders, the contrast is not about one being a more skilled designer, employing better construction teams, or using higher-quality materials. As far as we know, the two men were equals, with the exception of one major issue—the ground they were standing on. And that made all the difference.

The parable highlights our commitment to hear and act upon the words of Jesus. "Everyone who hears these words of mine." How's your hearing? When growing up, my wife's younger sister seemed to have a hearing problem. Her folks took her to an ear specialist who could find no physical problem. The doctor was perplexed, but little Sally solved the mystery when she innocently responded, "Sometimes my ears say yes and sometimes my ears say no." Could it be we don't always want to hear what the Lord has to say to us?

Did you notice what words Jesus is saying here? This parable is not inserted randomly into the text, but is the powerful conclusion to the most powerful sermon in Scripture—the Sermon on the Mount (Matthew 5–7). In the sermon, Jesus promotes new counter-cultural ideals for daily living: turn the other cheek, go the second mile, and pray for those who mistreat you; avoid anger, the seedbed of murder; avoid lust, the threshold to adultery; pray and fast in private, be salt and light in public; do ask, seek, knock; don't swear, judge, or worry. Radical stuff!

Some years ago I learned the necessity of a good foundation. Just after the footer for our new house had been poured, the weather changed—rain became the daily forecast. I was sorely frustrated by the continual delay, but the lousy weather turned out to be a blessing. The rain exposed a drainage problem in the ground that would have caused issues in the future. Common sense dictated that we add

YOUR SPIN

Have you checked your foundation lately?
1. My knowledge of the Bible is _____.
   (good/average/poor/miserable)

2. My understanding of God's worldview is _____.
   (good/adequate/what's a worldview?)

3. My source for truth is _____.
   (the Bible/philosophy/humanism/pop culture/
   there is no single source for truth)

4. My rationale for doing good deeds springs from _____.
   (Jesus/government/peer pressure/
   longing for a pat on the back)

extra tile, rock, and sealer. The plan worked—the foundation and basement remain dry. Sure, it cost more at the time, but a solid foundation is worth every penny.

If we listen carefully and follow the Lord's blueprint for our lives, our house will stand—no leakage, no matter what storms may come. The word of God provides the only guaranteed safe building blocks for our foundation. Starting on any other ground just doesn't make good sense.

It's Your Move!

At the close of your group time, let everyone have time to write down an answer to this question: Who do you believe Jesus is, and why are you sure what you believe is true?

Keep your answers someplace where they will be with you, wherever you go. You don't have to share your answers, but ask each other: Are you satisfied with your answer? Does it make sense to you? If anyone answers no, talk about what can be done to feel more secure in our foundations for belief.

Consider an apologetics (defense of the faith) study to help your small group gain a solid footing on the truth. It is vital that we know what we believe and why we believe it.

BONUS

The most exquisite house will be worthless if built on a faulty foundation. Use some common sense—start with the rock solid truth of Jesus and build from there.

POINT

Answers to page 13: 1. 116 years, 2. Ecuador, 3. Sheep, 4. Squirrel fur, 5. Dog, 6. Albert, 7. Crimson, 8. New Zealand

SCATTERGORIES:
Finding Contentment in Chaos

PART ONE—GAME ON

Object of the Game

THE GAME OF SCATTERGORIES group game pits your mind against the clock and the minds of everyone else in play. It's easy to get sidetracked when the timer is ticking. As you play the game, consider the focus of your life. How can you stay content and on course when the pressure is on?

Game Preparation

This is an easy game for a group of any size. Depending on how you play it (single players or teams), you may have to borrow or create extra category cards. Make sure you have plenty of answer sheets and pencils available. Choose a room where all who are participating can gather easily. If you like, throw down some *scatter* cushions, and everyone can snag a seat on the floor. No tables are necessary.

> "The main thing is to keep the main thing the main thing."
> —attributed to Stephen Covey

TAKE TURNS

Get to know each other a little better in a fun way. Let each person choose one of the categories below (or others you think up). Have the group list at least five items that fit the chosen category for each person (never mind about the beginning letters). Categories could include:

- Places I've lived/visited
- Bands/singers/music I love
- Favorite foods
- Things I've done for fun
- Things I worry about

Setting a mood for the game could include using letters of the alphabet on triangle shapes, reflecting the distinctive die used in the game. Or you could print out some typical category names on large pieces of paper and hang those up around the room. Or you could use a lot of scattered items, such as confetti, buttons, or colored stones, and spread those out on surfaces in your room. Open up that brain and see what jumps out—just like the picture on the box!

TRIVIA

*T*HE GAME OF SCATTERGORIES, *a relatively new game, was introduced to the world in 1988 and produced by Hasbro's Milton Bradley division. The fast-paced game was an instant success, which spawned a television game show of the same name. The NBC-produced show was hosted by Dick Clark, with Charlie Tuna as the announcer. Sadly, the TV version was an instant flop and was canned after only six months on the air. Sorry, Charlie! (You can find an episode on YouTube, if you are really interested.)*

The seemingly simple game—come up with words, all beginning with the same letter, to fit different categories in a certain period of time—can be quite difficult. It received the Mensa Best Mind Game Award in 1990. ESL teachers have been known to use the game as a tool to help their students increase their overall language knowledge.

Hasbro offers what they call a Game Tasters version of the game—an abbreviated edition in a can which introduces the buyer to game play without a large investment. For those who enjoy pitting wits against the computer, there is a SUPER SCATTERGORIES game available. Let me warn you, computers are good at this game. Play at your own risk—self-esteem hangs in the balance.

If you have never played Scattergories in any form, visit www.hasbro. com and try a free online demo to get a taste for this brain twister. It may give you a much-needed edge when your small group gathers to play.

Playing by the Rules

You can play this game as individuals, couples, or other team combinations. Make it a women-against-men contest, if you like. Each person plays his or her own list. Points earned by each player are added together to create a total team score. If you don't want a potential gender war, then create the two teams based on age, occupations, height, alphabetical name order, drawing straws, or any other clever way you can come up with.

Add more tension by decreasing the allotted answer time with each new list. Or, if you play with teams, flip a coin to see which team starts with ten bonus points and which starts ten points in the hole. Can the team in the hole catch up? If not, remember that's what happens in life when we lose that spirit of contentment—we're always in the hole!

As with many of the popular board games, Hasbro has sanctioned a couple unique versions, the most intriguing of which is THE GAME OF SCATTERGORIES BIBLE EDITION. This would be a perfect edition to use for your small group. However, if no one in your group has the Bible edition, let me suggest you create your own.

To keep it simple, make your game time a combination of both traditional and Bible categories. Use three category lists from the original game box and three from your own created Bible lists to comprise a complete game. You'll already have the game timer, score sheets, and the alphabetic icosahedron (Yes, that's the correct name for a twenty-sided geometric figure. Just wait till we get to TRIVIAL PURSUIT!). Game play is identical except for the alternate biblical category lists. Here is a sample list to spark your creativity:

1. Bible cities and towns
2. Old Testament prophets
3. Names of Bible women
4. Bible kings
5. Miracles
6. Occupations in the Bible
7. Names for God
8. Bible villains
9. Musical instruments
10. Holy days and festivals

It's Your Move—OUT LOUD

11. Places where Jesus walked
12. Sins
13. Christian virtues
14. Weapons in the Bible
15. Bodies of water

You can take it from here. Not only will the Bible categories make the game more interesting, you just might learn something new.

To Eat

Here's an idea to satisfy appetites while building around your scattered theme. Before you meet, perhaps at your previous small group session together, roll the SCATTERGORIES die and see what letter comes up. Then have each family or group member bring a different food item that begins with that letter. For example, a C might give you celery, cheese cubes, chips, cucumber slices, casserole, carrots, custard, chocolate anything, etc. Or the host for the meeting could choose his or her favorite snack-producing letter and assign items accordingly. Another idea might be to let everyone bring an item that begins with the same letter as his or her last name. The Quinceys, the Xaviers, and the Zanes may have lots of fun with that idea!

For Younger Players

Hasbro offers a junior edition of this group game, which is designed for kids, but this is an easy game to incorporate younger members in the fun. If you choose to play as family teams, the kids will add invaluable thoughts and words. Children are more creative than we often give them credit; and sometimes the hardest answers to come up with are the simplest words in the world. Let kids take turns being the official timekeeper. Kids enjoy operating the SCATTERGORIES timer.

Picking Up the Pieces

Our culture makes it difficult to be content. Did you ever notice how the volume on the television increases when a commercial airs? Every advertisement seems designed to make us restless. The old microwave with only forty-five power settings and a blah-white finish can't compare to the new stainless model with sixty-seven power settings. And did you ever try to pick out new paint colors? Talk about categories! I'm convinced there are more names for blue paint than there are actual shades of the color in the world.

So many things to do, places to go, people to please, products to buy, and goals to achieve—it's no wonder everyone is stressed to the max. Don't you think it's time to simplify—time to find contentment?

Read Luke 10:38 42 and think about Martha and Mary:

- Which one of these characters do you relate to the most?

- What lesson about a contented life can you learn from Jesus' response to Martha?

End the session by praying for one another to discover contentment as you:

- struggle to live daily in our consumer-driven culture.

- examine your goals and the ways to reach them.

- consider what might be distracting you from your relationship with God.

SCATTERGORIES:
Finding Contentment in Chaos

PART TWO—POSTGAME BREAKDOWN

Object of the Study

Time is short, the brain is always racing, chaos surrounds you, and you feel like your timer is about to go *click!* In all the commotion, God can help you find the key to calm.

Bible Content

The apostle Paul definitely had more than his share of ups and downs in his life. He could probably easily list items that would fill up a card of categories of punishments, trials, disasters, abuses, and hard times that all happened to him. Yet he still found joy in his lot and wanted to tell others about it:

> *I rejoice greatly in the Lord that at last you have renewed*
> *your concern for me. Indeed, you have been concerned, but*
> *you had no opportunity to show it. I am not saying this because*
> *I am in need, for I have learned to be content whatever the cir-*
> *cumstances. I know what it is to be in need, and I know what it*
> *is to have plenty. I have learned the secret of being content in*
> *any and every situation, whether well fed or hungry, whether*
> *living in plenty or in want. I can do everything through him*
> *who gives me strength.*
>
> —Philippians 4:10-13

To Study

I wonder how long it took Paul to learn contentment. Certainly, when he enters the story line of Acts, he is anything but content. Filled with a burning zeal, Saul (his name before his conversion) was driven to rid the world of this religious sect called Christianity. He bursts upon the scene as one bent on becoming a principal figure among the aristocratic Jewish leadership. Mr. Type A personality. The first-century alpha male. Not exactly the soul of contentment.

Discovering contentment in the midst of our complex culture can be a real challenge, no matter what kind of personality you are. Consider the following:

- Our lives are relationally complex—in addition to the traditional family unit, our society includes single-parent families, blended families, and intergenerational families, where grandparents are raising their grandkids. Children today can experience multiple marriages, joint custody, and extended family trees that branch in dozens of directions.

- Our careers are vocationally complex. Twenty percent of the country relocates annually; today's college grads will have ten different employers prior to retirement and will work in three different vocations.

- Our culture is financially complex. People are working extended hours at multiple jobs to meet basic financial obligations. The urge to splurge continues to surge as Americans spend most, if not all, of what they make. John DeGraaf, in his book *Affluenza: The All-Consuming Epidemic*, notes that American's average rate of saving in 1980 was 10 percent of earned income; that percentage has now dropped to zero. We expend 100 percent of take-home pay with debt. "We spend more on trash bags than 90 of the world's 210 countries spend for everything!" (from http://www.yhwh.com/Thoughts/FinancialHealth.htm).

- Our families are technologically complex. Most Americans have access to a computer and the Internet. In addition, many now carry cell phones, laptops, iPods, iPhones, Blackberries, MP3 players, and more. We e-mail, IM, chat, post, text, and Tweet. Strangers can learn, in one trip

TAKE A TURNS

1. Do you think it's better to focus on thankful actions, or thankful attitudes? Why?

2. What kinds of acts create the greatest amounts of gratitude?

3. What do you think about the statement: "True contentment begins with genuine thanks"? What do you think is the link between contentment and gratitude?

YOUR↗SPIN

1. Think about a time in the recent past when you felt extremely relieved. Did that feeling produce thankfulness in you? If so, how did you act on that?

2. Is thankfulness an occasional action for you, or a habitual attitude? What helps you remember to be thankful?

3. How much does gratitude impact your personal contentment level on a daily basis?

to your Facebook account, more than you may want them to know. Your daughter can now sell her Girl Scout cookies via her own Web site while your son sells your old baseball card collection on eBay. Technology changes daily; information explodes at a frightening pace.

It wears me out just thinking of life's complexity; is there any comfort in the chaos? Check out Paul's advice to the Philippian Christians.

BE THANKFUL FOR EVERY GIFT

Paul's letter to the Philippians is in part a thank-you note, although he never uses the expression "thank you." As a Roman prisoner, Paul had no means of financial support. The Philippian church took it upon themselves to help with his financial needs. Up to that point they had no opportunity to demonstrate their concern—most likely because couriers between Philippi and Rome were few and far between. While these gifts were joyfully received by Paul, his

"Multiple times every day, we do the computational equivalent of fully exploring every intersection of every road in the United States. Except it'd be a map about 50,000 times as big as the U.S., with 50,000 times as many roads and intersections."
—Jesse Alpert & Nissan Hajaj on mapping the Web, The Official Google Blog, July 25, 2008

1. Why is it difficult for us to slow down?

2. What would you have to give up to slow down, move over, and cheer up?

3. When do you take time to take stock of what you have? How does this change your thinking?

deepest gratitude was reserved for the Philippians themselves. Their partnership with him in ministry meant more than any food, clothing, or money they could have sent. Who could forget the way Paul began his letter: "I thank my God every time I remember you." (1:3) True contentment begins with genuine thanks.

BE CONTENT IN EVERY SITUATION

Paul told his friends, "I have learned the secret of being content in any and every situation" (Philippians 4:12). That may seem like a pretty grand claim, but it's not so hard to believe if you think about the things Paul had gone through, and been rescued from. Contentment follows an awareness of gratitude.

Professional golfer, Paul Azinger, had his world turned upside down when he was diagnosed with cancer. His treatments were successful and he returned to the PGA tour, but he returned a changed man. Azinger made this observation, "I've made a lot of money since I've been on the tour, and I've won a lot of tournaments, but that happiness is always temporary. The only way you will ever have true contentment is in a personal relationship with Jesus Christ. I'm not saying that nothing ever bothers me and I don't have problems, but I feel like I've found the answer to the six-foot hole" (Paul Azinger with Ken Abraham, *Zinger*, Zondervan, 1996).

So how do you make yourself more aware of, and more thankful for, what you have? Consider three simple actions.

Slow down. One of my favorite episodes of *The Andy Griffith Show* is "Sermon for Today." Guest minister from the big city of New York, Dr. Breen, delivers a message about slowing down. Here is an excerpt of his, uh, stirring sermon:

> Why this senseless rush, this mad pursuit, this frantic competition, this pace that kills? Why do we drive ourselves as we do? . . . Consider how we live our lives today; everything is run, run, run! We bolt our breakfast, we scan the headlines, we race to the office. A full schedule and the split second—these are our gauges of success. We drive ourselves from morn to night. My friends, we've forgotten the meaning of the word, "Relaxation!" . . . And so I say to you, dear friends: Relax, slow down, take it easy. What's your hurry? What, indeed, friends, is your hurry?

Your life won't be simple by accident; you must make a concerted effort to balance the pace of your schedule. So slow down, take it easy. What's your hurry?

Move over. Let the proverbial Joneses go on ahead. Life is not a competition to see who can accumulate the most whatevers. Live within your means, avoid chasing after someone else's dreams, and don't use the Joneses, the Smiths, or the Rockefellers as the standard for what you should have. Let God be your standard. Debt and disappointment are twin bullies that will beat the contentment right out of you. Move over and let them pass you by.

"It is right to be contented with what we have, never with what we are."
—James Mackintosh

Cheer up. Do you know the result of the rat race? Somebody wins, somebody loses—but we all end up as rats. Few people seem happy in the midst of chaos. Got a pessimist lurking inside of you? Find an empty grave and bury him! Cultivate a positive outlook, find ways to laugh more, and spend your resources on relationships rather than real estate. Put others first and you may be surprised how content you become.

BE STEADFAST EVERY DAY

Life is not like your DVR or video player—you can't fast-forward through the bad parts. The tough episodes play out in real time just like the good, but keep in mind that regardless of the theme, Jesus is present in every scene. How else could Paul write such inspirational words of contentment in a dank prison cell?

"I can do everything through him who gives me strength." Your faith may be challenged on a daily basis—in plenty or in want. But don't forget, you too, can do everything through Christ who gives you strength.

While in India, I had the privilege of preaching for a congregation in the city of Sagar. Before the evening service, the preacher and his wife took me to the small piece of property the church had purchased, where they dreamed of constructing a church building. Their eyes lit up as they spoke with excitement and conviction about their work for Christ in that university town. After returning to the U.S., I learned that a few weeks later the preacher's neighbors lied about him to the local police. The officers took him to the marketplace and, in front of a large hotel, beat him for the better part of an hour. Following that brutal attack, he was unable to walk for quite some time. And yet, he is steadfast in preaching Jesus, and the congregation grows. What keeps him going? It's the knowledge that he can do everything through the strength of Christ.

YOUR SPIN

Analyze your personal contentment. Answer with true or false:

1. I am generally a cheerful person. _____

2. I often dream of living a different life. _____

3. I panic when things go wrong. _____

4. I can be happy when others get a nice gift and I get nothing. _____

5. I express my thanksgiving to God and others on a daily basis. _____

6. I rarely complain. _____

7. My friends would say I live a consistent life. _____

It's Your Move!

Go through your boxes, trunks, closets, attics, basements, sheds, rented storage units, and get rid of the stuff you don't need or never use. Try this rule of thumb: if it hasn't been used, worn, or played with for a year or two, pitch it. As a small group, hold a multi-family garage sale and give all the proceeds to a missionary supported by your local congregation. Box up the unsold items from the garage sale and offer them to a local charity that will make your donation available to those who have needs.

Rework your schedule. Set aside time daily to read the Bible, pray, and do something just for fun. Your fun thing may be reading a novel or going for a walk in the woods. Too tame, you say? Then try something with a higher thrill rate—way higher. Can you spell s-k-y-d-i-v-i-n-g? Find what refreshes you and restores your joy. Start now to simplify.

BONUS

Contentment and simplicity grow out of a relationship with Christ, not out of an absence of crisis. Anything can be done through him who gives us strength.

POINT

PICTIONARY:

Grasping God's Vision

PART ONE—GAME ON

Object of the Game

As you draw your way to victory, imagine the challenge God faced in effectively communicating his vision to us. How do you show his story to others?

Game Preparation

Only one game set will be needed as this is a perfect game for a group of any size. While you can use a dry-erase white board or chalkboard for drawing, I would recommend two large flip pads, two easels, and a variety of colored markers (preferably nonpermanent ink). Flip pads, available at most office supply stores, are more convenient and less messy. Why two? Each team will need one for the All Play cards. The easels will enhance both visibility and game play.

> "Vision is looking at life through the lens of God's eye."
> —Anonymous

To create a PICTIONARY game mood, make two kinds of posters: 1) Posters resembling the playing cards, listing an item for each of the following categories (you can just copy the items from a card in the pack, or make up your own):

- Person/Place/Animal (names included).

- Object (can be touched or seen).

- Action (a thing that can be done).

- Difficult (challenging word).

- All Play (any type of word).

2) Posters with sample sketches or drawings that depict each of the words you have printed on the card posters.

*B*ack in the early 1980s, Rob Angel worked as a waiter in Seattle, Washington. It was just a job; but while he served tables, his mind was serving up an idea for a new game. It all began to take shape as, in a loose game format, he started sketching illustrations of dictionary words at parties. His party game was so popular he developed the board game version and promoted it first by selling sets door-to-door. Since 1985, the PICTIONARY game has become a national favorite, with several editions and two attempts at creating a television game show of the same name.

Playing by the Rules

I highly recommend a two-team competition for this game. The rules state that up to four teams can play; but for your Game On session, two will be more enjoyable. You can use a traditional method for dividing up teams (men vs. women, drawing straws, by age, etc.) but since this is a picture-word game, try something more picturesque. Cut slips of paper equal to the number in your group. On half of the slips, write the name Picasso, and on the other half, Monet. Fold the slips up and place them in a container and let every player pick a slip. You now have two teams with artistic flair for added inspiration.

With fifty-six color squares on the board and 3,000 words to choose from, you won't run out of pictures to draw.

The Bible edition of the PICTIONARY game is no longer sold, but you can easily create Bible-themed cards on your own. Do this as a group. Before the game playing begins, have each team quietly craft five cards using specific Bible terms for each of the categories. Place the cards facedown and swap them so each team is using the cards created by the other. Everyone on the team must take a turn at being the picturist (the official title for the one drawing the clues.)

Looking for a way to make the game more challenging? Try these ideas:
- Once the clue word has been viewed, blindfold the picturist! You'll be amazed how difficult it is to create clues without the mouth or the eyes.

- Have the picturist use his or her nondominant hand to draw—that should produce a few chuckles. In this adaptation, you can only hope the ambidextrous family is on your team.

- Try this: when the picturist is drawing the clues, the marker cannot be lifted from the paper. More thought will go into the clue if the picture has no line breaks.

To Eat

Provide snacks that represent the categories of the game:

- Person/Place/Animal—Foods known by place, person, or animal name. For example: Boston cream pie, Orville Redenbacher popcorn, California raisins, Puppy Chow (see recipe).

- Object—Foods you can eat with your fingers: apple slices, bananas, celery sticks with cheese spread or peanut butter, hard-boiled eggs, chips and dip, etc.

- Action—Foods that have a verb in their name: snap peas, pull-apart bread, turnovers, baked beans, tossed salads, etc.

- Difficult—Foods spelled with unique words: artichoke hearts, avocado dip, rutabaga casserole, minestrone soup, Wiener Schnitzel, etc.

- If that cuisine doesn't work for your small group, offer multi-ingredient dishes that are somewhat ambiguous, such as casseroles or hard-to-recognize salads. Each dish should be labeled with a hand-drawn picture card only—use no words, written or verbal—that reflects either the specific name of the dish (meatloaf surprise) or the ingredients (broccoli, cheese, and cream of celery soup). Place each card in front of its dish. Then let the guessing begin!

For Younger Players

Obviously, PICTIONARY JUNIOR is a viable option for the younger set, but this is a game where the whole family can participate. Include the kids on your team. You might be surprised—the younger team members might just be the best guessers and sketchers.

As you play the game, you might want to point out things that make getting the right answer hard:

- too complicated drawing.
- someone not being familiar with the clue item.
- failing to use common knowledge to help create an image.

MIX IT UP

½ CUP PEANUT BUTTER	9 CUPS RICE CEREAL SQUARES
¼ CUP BUTTER	1 ½ CUPS CONFECTIONER'S
1 CUP CHOCOLATE CHIPS	SUGAR

Melt the peanut butter, butter, and chocolate chips together, either in a microwave-safe bowl or in a saucepan. Stir well. Pour the cereal in a large bowl. Pour the melted mixture over the cereal and mix all well. When cereal is well mixed, sprinkle sugar over it, adding a bit at a time and mixing the cereal after each addition in order to have every piece of cereal coated very well.

Picking Up the Pieces

Throughout the Bible, God communicated with humanity in a variety of ways: dreams, visions, theophanies, miracles, prophecies, revelation, and command- ments. The message didn't always sink in. Then, in a stroke of genius, God decided to give us more than words; he gave us a living picture! He became totally human— one of us—in order that we might see and experience his message of grace. Seeing is believing.

What can you learn about God and his vision for this world by studying the life of his Son? If a pic- ture paints a thousand words, then the life of Christ painted volumes about the love of God. Jesus gives dimension and depth to the words of Scripture.

His vision for us is that we share his pic- ture with those who need to know him. Have you grasped God's vision?

> "Vision encompasses vast vistas outside the realm of the predictable, the safe, the expected. No wonder we perish without it!"
>
> —Charles R. Swindoll, *The Tale of the Tardy Oxcart*

Read Acts 3:1-10. When Peter and John healed the lame man, there were consequences.

- List the result of their efforts to live out God's vision for their lives. What did it cost them?

- Now read Acts 4:13. What is the source of your courage?

- What are you willing to give up in order to grasp God's vision?

Close with prayer. Ask God to fill your group with the courage and ability of the first-century Christians to:

- grasp God's vision.

- communicate God's vision.

- live out God's vision.

TAKE TURNS

1. After playing the game, take a vote: Who were the best artists? That is, which people in your group drew well? Now, who were the most successful artists? That is, who won the most points for their teams? Talk about what qualities make it easy or hard to grasp the idea someone is presenting. Consider how getting people to see an idea often takes more than one kind of talent.

2. At what level of faith do you believe most Christians grasp God's vision for the church? for their individual lives? How would you draw God's vision? Grab paper and a pencil—give it your best shot.

PICTIONARY:

Grasping God's Vision

Object of the Study

God wants us to have clarity when it comes to his plan and purpose for our lives. Throughout Scripture the Lord has drawn hundreds of word pictures so that we might visualize his story from beginning to end. Grasping God's story gives us clear vision for each new day.

Bible Content

For additional preparation and insight, I recommend you read Joshua 2, 5, and 6.

> The men said to her, "This oath you made us swear will not
> be binding on us unless, when we enter the land, you have
> tied this scarlet cord in the window through which you let us
> down, and unless you have brought your father and mother,
> your brothers and all your family into your house. If anyone
> goes outside your house into the street, his blood will be on
> his own head; we will not be responsible. As for anyone who
> is in the house with you, his blood will be on our head if a
> hand is laid on him. But if you tell what we are doing, we will
> be released from the oath you made us swear." "Agreed," she
> replied. "Let it be as you say." So she sent them away and they
> departed. And she tied the scarlet cord in the window.
>
> —Joshua 2:17-21

> Then they burned the whole city and everything in it, but
> they put the silver and gold and the articles of bronze and iron
> into the treasury of the Lord's house. But Joshua spared Rahab
> the prostitute, with her family and all who belonged to her,
> because she hid the men Joshua had sent as spies to Jericho—
> and she lives among the Israelites to this day.
>
> —Joshua 6:24, 25

To Study

Before we explore Rahab's drama, let me set the stage. The seemingly random events of the Bible are not random at all, but a carefully orchestrated journal of God's vision through the ages. Every major biblical moment is strung together like a strand of Christmas lights, all illuminating the one special purpose of his story.

Unfortunately, too many people misunderstand God's vision. In the spring of 2009, the Indiana Atheist Bus Campaign's slogan "You Can Be Good Without God" popped up in various places. If the slogan was intended to contradict God's story, it missed the point of his vision. Christianity is not some self-help, social organization that provides us motivation to be good. In actuality none of us, Christian or atheist, can genuinely be good. We all can do good, but being good is another matter. Our inability to be good is the very reason for God's story.

TAKE TURNS

1. Many of us, if not all, have at one time or another read an illustrated Bible storybook. What pictures from such a book were most memorable to you, and why?

2. What pictures in your life have stood out to you as illustrating God's hand on you or those around you?

3. Open any newspaper or Web news item and you will soon see some picture (whether in words or photos) of sin's effects on humankind. What effect do such images have on you? Why do you think people are generally more intrigued with such stories than those of kindness, love, or generosity?

Think about some images from your own life.

1. When were you first aware of sin in your life? What did your relationship with Jesus look like then?

2. Picture a time when sin had its hold on you. What did your relationship with Jesus look like then?

3. Consider a time in your life when you felt freed from a particular sin, or from the enslavement of sin in general. What did your relationship with Jesus look like then?

OUR SCARLET CURSE

"'Come now, let us reason together,' says the LORD. 'Though your sins are like scarlet, they shall be as white as snow; though they are red as crimson, they shall be like wool'" (Isaiah 1:18). From the very beginning, humanity has struggled with the devastation of sin. Black often depicts the color of sin, but red may be a better choice. When's the last time you saw a picture of Satan in pink tights holding a powder-blue pitchfork? Red is the color of the dragon in Revelation that symbolizes the devil. Red is the color of fire, the ultimate punishment for Satan and sin. Red warns of danger. Red is the facial tint of rage. Red is the color of the light that shines from a window, enticing a lonely man into the arms of a woman who sells her body.

It all started at that tree—the fruit of which God had instructed Adam not to eat (Genesis 2 and 3). I don't know if the fruit of that tree was red, but from there, sin's scarlet scourge has raced through every book and chapter. Cain killed his brother Abel, and Abel's crimson blood cried out from the ground for justice. Noah got drunk, Abraham lied, Jacob deceived, Tamar seduced, Moses murdered, Aaron idolized, Samson weakened, Saul disobeyed, David lusted, Solomon lost faith, Elijah despaired, and Jonah ran.

It got no better in the New Testament. Regarding Jesus, King Herod sought his death, the Pharisees plotted his death, and Pilate allotted his death. Judas betrayed him, Peter denied him, and Thomas doubted him. Paul persecuted his church, Ananias and Sapphira cheated his church, Simon the sorcerer extorted his church, and Demas abandoned his church.

We are part of a long line of folks whose sins have left crimson blotches on the pages of God's history. We all suffer under the scarlet curse.

HIS SCARLET CORD

Only God can remove such a curse. And for our scarlet curse, he has a scarlet cure. God's vision for that remedy goes back again to a conversation in the Garden of Eden. "And I will put enmity between you and the woman, and between your offspring and hers; he will crush your head, and you will strike his heel" (Genesis 3:15).

TAKE TURNS

Play Telephone PICTIONARY. Have several people sit in a row, all facing one way, so no one sees the person behind. Give each person a small pad of paper and a marker. The leader chooses a phrase or an action to be drawn: washing an elephant, shooting the breeze, basting the turkey, etc. The leader taps the first player, who turns around and watches the leader draw out the phrase. Each person will have thirty seconds to draw. At the end of the thirty seconds, the watcher turns around, taps the next person in line (who turns around to watch), and draws out what they think the phrase is. This continues down the line. The last person in line then must guess the phrase.

After you play (and are finished laughing at the result), talk about how the picture we paint of God can get garbled, and what we can do to ensure our messages about God and his love are clear.

Check your visionary potential. Rate yourself on a scale of 1 to 5; 1 being "never," and 5 being "almost all the time."

1. I go out on a limb for things I really believe in. _____
2. When I fail at something, I try again. _____
3. When bad things happen, I still trust that God is good. _____
4. I rely on God's Word to know how to live my life. _____
5. Whenever I'm in doubt, the first thing I do is pray. _____

It was there God wove his scarlet cord into the tapestry of human history. From that first promise of a coming Savior, the vision reached its climax on the final day of Christ's life: "Then the governor's soldiers took Jesus into the Praetorium and gathered the whole company of soldiers around him. They stripped him and put a scarlet robe on him, and then twisted together a crown of thorns and set it on his head. . . . Then they led him away to crucify him" (Matthew 27:27-29, 31).

But let's back up a bit and pick up the thread at a different spot. Before the Israelites crossed the Jordan to conquer the promised land, Joshua sent two trusted spies to scope out Jericho. The spies didn't blend in and were soon being hunted. They took refuge at Rahab's place; a prostitute's house that was literally in the wall of Jericho. She saved the spies by hiding them on her roof, but before lowering them down by a scarlet cord, she pleaded with them to save her family. The spies instructed her to hang the scarlet cord in the window, and on the day of reckoning everyone in her house would be spared. Each day until the Israelites marched against Jericho, that scarlet cord hung in the window as a testimony to her faith. On the seventh day, with a shout and trumpet blast, the wall came tumbling down. But Rahab and her family were saved.

God's vision for grace is often greater than our ability to grasp it. Rahab was faced with fear on all sides—the king of Jericho himself was putting pressure on her to reveal the spies. And on the other hand, the spies were with the army of the Lord, whom the people of her city feared so much that she said, "Our hearts melted and everyone's courage failed because of you" (Joshua 2:11). Rahab could have caved under the threat of punishment that would surely have come to her for the betrayal of her city, but instead she literally looked beyond the walls and put her faith in God's plan, "for the Lord your God is God in heaven above and on the earth below." Rahab grasped the vision, at least, for the security of her family.

And her part in God's story did not end there. The pagan prostitute became a follower of God, embraced the Jewish faith, and married a Jewish man, Salmon. Together they had a son named Boaz, who had a son named Jesse, who had a son named David. Rahab was the great-grandmother of King David—the scarlet cord wound itself around her family and right straight down the genealogy of Jesus Christ. The security of Rahab's family that day in Jericho meant something to the family of God.

Throughout Scripture God shows us picture after picture of how he has enabled salvation for his people:

- Noah listened to God and everyone in the ark was saved.

- The Israelites obeyed God and were saved in their houses, passed over by the angel of death.

- Moses followed God and everyone who passed through the Red Sea was saved.

- Jesus obeyed, even to death, and now "Everyone who calls on the name of the Lord will be saved" (Romans 10:13).

TAKE TURNS

1. What are some simple ways you can encourage others to grasp the vision of God?

2. Describe an experience when you shared God's story with someone. Would you do it any differently if you had the chance? Why or why not?

And what did Rahab do to be saved? Was it because of her exemplary lifestyle? Was it because she lied to the men who came looking for the spies? Was it because she tied a scarlet cord in her window?

"By faith the prostitute Rahab, because she welcomed the spies, was not killed with those who were disobedient" (Hebrews 11:31).

Rahab believed in the God of heaven and earth, and she believed that if the men swore by their Lord to do her kindness, then kindness would be done.

Are you getting the vision now? God wants his people to be saved; and to be saved, his people have to believe.

It's Your Move!

How can your small group live out God's vision for your lives? How can you help communicate his story to others?

- Offer to help your church host a one-day seminar on how to share your personal faith in our twenty-first-century culture.

- Check with local benevolence agencies about supplying back-to-school items for needy children. Provide backpacks with folders, notebooks, pencils, pens, crayons, etc.—no strings attached. Include with each backpack a children's Bible or Bible storybook and some information about your church's ministries.

- Host a cookout for your neighbors. If they are strangers to you or only casual acquaintances, this can be your first move in building a genuine relationship—a relationship that may open the door for you to help them see God's vision for their lives.

BONUS

It's not about being good, it's about finding the one who is. God's vision is within your grasp. When you see the scarlet cord of his grace, follow it and it will lead you all the way home.

POINT

TRIVIAL PURSUIT:
Checking Your Priorities

PART ONE—GAME ON

Object of the Game

Is your brain cluttered with vast amounts of useless information? If so, this game may come easy for you. As you play, take some time to reflect on your priorities: Which pieces of your pie are most important, and which ones are truly trivial?

Game Preparation

Depending on the size of your group, and whether or not you decide to play as teams, you will need at least two TRIVIAL PURSUIT game boards, as there are only six players per game. Use identical versions or mix it up and give group members a choice.

> "Time has a wonderful way of weeding out the trivial."
>
> —Richard Ben Sapir, Quest

Here are some trivial and not-so-trivial ideas for creating an atmosphere for the game:

- Decorate with the six colors represented by the categories of questions: blue, pink, yellow, brown, green, and orange.

- Make a mobile of six pie wedge shapes representing the categories and suspend it above the playing table(s).

- Hang banners around the room highlighting the six categories of: Geography, Entertainment, History, Art & Literature, Science & Nature, and Sports & Leisure.

- Post trivial questions around the room to spark discussions as group members gather. Have the answers available after the game is over.

Have enough paper and pens available for the Trivial Food Challenge (see To Eat section for details). Provide one chef's hat for the winner.

On December 15, 1979, friends Chris Haney and Scott Abbott got together in Montreal, Canada, for a game of SCRABBLE. Fortunately for us, their set was missing some pieces, so in their disappointment they began to explore the idea of creating their own game. That was no insignificant discussion—the end product turned out to be TRIVIAL PURSUIT. Parker Brothers (now part of Hasbro) bought the rights to market it in the United States, and in 1984 alone, a record-breaking twenty million games were sold. In 1993, Games magazine named TRIVIAL PURSUIT to the Games Hall of Fame (http://www.ideafinder.com/history/inventions/trivialpursuit.htm).

There is nothing trivial about the variety of versions of the game that are available today. The Hasbro Web site lists more than sixty results for a search of TRIVIAL PURSUIT games. In addition to the original, you can play the following editions: 25th Anniversary, Family, 80s, Pop Culture, Commercials, and more. Hasbro offers a Junior edition, a Nickelodeon edition and several DVD editions all for the younger set. More than most board games, this one has invaded the electronic world as well. The game is available for your DVD player, computer, Playstation, Xbox, Wii, iPod, iPhone, iTouch, mobile phone—and there's a free online version. Whew! You now have access to more trivial information than you would ever want to pursue.

Playing by the Rules

Playing by the set of rules that are included can be quite challenging, but if the standard rules are just too trivial for you, here's an idea to make game play more interesting.

Instead of playing as individuals, play as teams, or families. The families can be actual families that are part of your group, or you can create "families" by dividing everyone up. One way to do this would be to put a number of pie pieces in a bag or hat—make sure you have enough for the number in your whole group, and make sure there are equal numbers of each color, as much as possible. Then let players draw for pie pieces; all the pinks will be a family, all the greens will be a family, and so on.

Each family will then play as one unit—and you can include the kids as well. Every other turn, the question should be answered collectively; the family can confer on a response. On the alternate turns the question must be answered by an individual without team assistance. The answer giver must be identified before the question is asked. Here's the kicker; everyone on the team must answer at least one question in the game. When a child is called upon to answer, use question cards from a junior edition. A team cannot be declared the winner until each family member has answered at least one question.

To Eat

If you've ever thought about serving some unusual or unique dishes, now would be the time. Got an old family recipe that no one would recognize? Dust it off and get it ready for the small group. Each individual or family should bring a treat, but the name and ingredients should be kept a secret. Disguise the dish however is needed, but simply identify each food item with a number card.

TAKE TURNS

Have everyone take a pie or draw a pie (circle). Talk about these questions.

1. If your pie represents everything you do in a week, show how much of your time in a usual week would be taken up with what you would consider trivial pursuits.

2. What would you have to do to reclaim some of that time and devote it to more significant projects? Are there any of those trivial things that are actually accomplishing important acts (for example: playing golf with a grieving friend in order to take their mind off stressful things)?

Before the game begins, but after everyone has had a chance to sample the fare, grab pen and paper to compete for the title of Chief Chef in the Trivial Food Challenge. Next to the corresponding food number, record everything you know (or think you know) about that particular treat. The person who can identify the most recipe names, foods, or ingredients correctly can be celebrated as Chief Chef. The prize—a chef's hat that must be worn during the Trivial Pursuit game and a second helping of the winner's favorite food.

Here's a unique recipe just to get your creative juices flowing.

1 BOX YELLOW CAKE MIX

1 BOX INSTANT VANILLA PUDDING

4 BEATEN EGGS

¾ CUP OIL

1 10 OZ. CAN OF DR. PEPPER
COLA DRINK

¾ CUPS CHOPPED WALNUTS
(OPTIONAL)

GLAZE: 1 CUP POWDERED SUGAR AND
1 TSP VANILLA AND DR. PEPPER
DRINK—USE AMOUNT NEEDED
FOR DESIRED CONSISTENCY.

Preheat oven to 350 degrees F. Grease a bundt pan. Mix all ingredients together well (except for glaze) and pour into the pan. Bake for one hour. Take cake out, remove from pan, and let it cool. Mix ingredients together for the glaze. Add Dr. Pepper gradually to the sugar and vanilla, mixing until you achieve desired consistency. It shouldn't be too watery or too thick. When cake is cooled, pour glaze over the top of the cake.

For Younger Players

If your group elects to play individually by the original rules, then you may wish to provide one of the junior editions of the game for the kids. If your group has only one or two children, let them be the distributors of the wedge pieces for correct answers or keepers of the question cards. In that way they can participate in the game excitement even though the questions will most likely be beyond their scope of knowledge.

Talk to them about what *trivial* means and how it's good to *pursue* important goals, rather than chase after meaningless ones.

Picking Up the Pieces

When you stop to think about it, many of life's choices are rather trivial: the color of your vehicle, button-down or buttonless shirt collars, matte or glossy photos, generic or brand-name pharmaceuticals, anti-bacterial or regular soap—the list seems endless. However, there is one area of life where our choices truly matter. There is nothing trivial about the choices we make when it comes to our spiritual relationship with the Lord.

King Saul learned that lesson the hard way; it cost him his crown and the favor of God. Read 1 Samuel 15 and discuss the choices that Saul made throughout the ordeal with the Amalekites.

- How does the conversation between Samuel and King Saul shape your understanding of sacrifice?

- Why do you think obedience is so important to God? Why in particular would it have been important for Saul to show his ability to obey?

- How can a correct understanding of God's expectation of obedience help you make decisions about your priorities?

Close with a time of prayer; ask God to help you discern how you can change your life to better:

- distinguish between the important and the trivial.

- make time for the significant relationships in your life.

- avoid getting wrapped up in the mundane.

TRIVIAL PURSUIT:
Checking Your Priorities

PART TWO—POSTGAME BREAKDOWN

Object of the Study

The amount of knowledge available at one's fingertips today is staggering. But all knowledge is not wisdom. Set your priorities according to God's wisdom. Remember the words of Proverbs 1:7: "The fear of the Lord is the beginning of knowledge, but fools despise wisdom and discipline."

Bible Content

Jesus replied: "A certain man was preparing a great banquet and invited many guests. At the time of the banquet he sent his servant to tell those who had been invited, 'Come, for everything is now ready.'

"But they all alike began to make excuses. The first said, 'I have just bought a field, and I must go and see it. Please excuse me.'

"Another said, 'I have just bought five yoke of oxen, and I'm on my way to try them out. Please excuse me.'

"Still another said, 'I just got married, so I can't come.'

"The servant came back and reported this to his master. Then the owner of the house became angry and ordered his servant, 'Go out quickly into the streets and alleys of the town and bring in the poor, the crippled, the blind and the lame.'

"'Sir,' the servant said, 'what you ordered has been done, but there is still room.'

"Then the master told his servant, 'Go out to the roads and country lanes and make them come in, so that my house will be full. I tell you, not one of those men who were invited will get a taste of my banquet.'"

—Luke 14:16-24

To Study

How do your priorities stack up against the Lord's expectations? Let's take a look at the parable Jesus told as we think about this question.

GOD'S CALL IS NOT A TRIVIAL INVITATION

This is no ordinary summons. A banquet of this scope would have been the social event of the year for any Jewish community of Jesus' day. No clear-headed, thoughtful recipient would have dismissed such a coveted invitation, and yet, some in the parable did. Apparently they considered their business more important. How do we determine what matters and what does not?

Consider who extends the invitation. A challenge to meet a friend on the course for a round of golf does not carry the same weight as a meeting request from the principal of your child's school, or perhaps a dinner invitation from your boss.

In the parable, the host of the feast represents the Lord, whose invitation to his kingdom should come at the top of any priority register. Amazingly, as in the parable, there are those who simply aren't interested. Caught up in the good things of life, it's as if the Lord's banquet becomes just one of several good places to eat. Tragically, it's not one of many; it's the only spiritual feast!

TAKE TURNS

1. Is the Lord's invitation to salvation really open to everyone? Even to those who've ignored it before? What do you think?

2. What was the Lord's invitation to Peter, Andrew, James and John as they cleaned their nets along the shore of the Sea of Galilee? (Matthew 4:18-22) How did they respond? What do you think compelled them to respond the way they did?

3. Turn to Luke 9:57-62 and read the response of others who received invitations. How do their responses compare to those of the fishermen? Which of these most closely represents your usual response to the things God wants you to do?

Consider the reason for the invitation. The parable's host was throwing a once-in-a-lifetime party and wanted his banquet hall full of guests. A generous man, he continually dispatched couriers into the community and countryside to compel people to attend. How could the people be so cavalier about such a grand invitation? The Lord wants his house full. His relational nature longs to extend grace and fill every seat at his eternal banquet table. How can we ignore his desires?

YOUR ↗ SPIN

Take a look at this list of excuses. Check off the ones you've used in the past week. How many have you used to put off doing something that would help you grow in your relationship with God? your relationship with others?

1. I'll get to it after I get my work finished.
2. I'm too tired—it's been a bad week.
3. I'm just not feeling up to it today—ask me tomorrow.
4. I'm not really cut out for that—it's not my thing.
5. I don't have enough resources to accomplish that just now.
6. There are many other people able to do that. Why not ask one of them?

CHARACTER IS NOT A TRIVIAL ISSUE

When it comes to character, we all start on a level playing field. Character is not determined by one's spiritual gifts, above-average intelligence, or highly developed skills; it springs from one's will and desire to reflect God's goodness.

I heard about a disheartened businessman who lost most of his financial investments. Being good friends with his minister, he decided to unload his frustration:

> He started with the words "I've lost everything," but got no further.

> "Character may be manifested in the great moments, but it is made in the small ones."
> —Phillips Brooks, author and minister

"I'm so sorry to hear you have lost your family," his friend interrupted.

"I didn't say I lost my family."

"Oh! Then I'm sorry to hear you have lost your character."

"I didn't say that either."

"Well, it must be a spiritual issue—I'm sorry to hear you have lost your faith."

By that point in the conversation, the businessman was beginning to catch on. He responded quietly, "I didn't lose my faith."

The minister smiled, "You have your family, your character, and your faith in God. It seems to me that you've lost none of the things which really matter."

Consider these ways to maintain the priority of character:

- Count the cost.

- Keep your commitments.

- Minimize the excuses.

Count the cost. Being a man or woman of character may cost you a relationship—if a friend urges you to participate in something that will compromise your integrity. Character may cost you a business deal—if the customer wants you to cheat. Character may cost you an invitation—from a coworker who wants to have an affair with you. It's true, character is costly, but in the long run it saves you more. It will save a true friendship, it will save your reputation in the business world, and it will save you the heartache of a broken family. Count the cost— character is worth the price.

Keep your commitments. I'm always amazed at people's level of commitment to seemingly insignificant priorities. Dr. Dale Glenn, in his book on the history of the Indiana High School Athletic Association, relates an incident at the Huntingburg basketball sectional tournament during my senior year. Being at every sectional game was a priority for many in the community. While a tournament game was in progress, an emergency call echoed over the public address system for a ticket holder to report to the gymnasium office. At the office, the man was greeted by the police and informed that his car had been doused with gasoline and set on fire. Glancing at action on the playing floor, the man inquired about the extent of the damage:

"It's a total loss," the officers responded.

The owner sighed as if relieved. "Well there's no sense going out there now," and he returned to his seat to finish watching the game. Now that's a true fan!

I wish a similar level of commitment was as obvious in those of us who wear the name of Christ. In the parable, the original invitees declined to honor their commitment at the time of the feast. How rude and inconsiderate! I learned to appreciate this parable even more when my daughters got married. As the reception RSVPs were returned, it dawned on me that if the responders decided not to attend at the last minute, I still had to pay for their meals. It gave me a new appreciation for the parable's host. No wonder he was frustrated. Commitments matter; especially the ones we make to God!

Minimize the excuses. In the parable, the reasons offered for not attending were not spiteful, but they were incredibly lame. One had bought some land and had to go look at it. (Was the land going somewhere?) Another had bought five teams of oxen and claimed he needed to try them out. (With ten new oxen, surely he could afford to have someone do that for him.) A new groom rejected the party, claiming family obligation. (I wonder what his new bride would have thought about his passing up the chance to take her to a rich dinner out?) All were excuses that pertained to relevant human concerns: property, money, and family. But all the excuses were empty. A person of true character does not rely on excuses, but despises them.

TAKE 🎲 TURNS

1. What are the attributes of a good character?

2. Why does character matter? Would you knowingly do business with a person of questionable character? Why or why not?

3. Do you consider it a priority to work on improving your character? If so, what do you do to help build up your character?

1. Consider a time when you missed a chance to do something you really wanted to do. What were the consequences? How did you feel?

2. How intentional are you with your time? Are you a planner? Or do you just take things as they come?

3. If you are a planner, consider blocking out a period of time where you have nothing to do. Go for a walk or a drive somewhere during this time and just keep an eye out for opportunities you might not have seen otherwise. If you are a more free-spirited person, plan to do an important thing that you have been putting off. Don't let anything get in your way. Just focus on doing the thing.

CONSEQUENCES ARE NOT A TRIVIAL CONCERN

Those who had been invited but failed to attend did not get a second chance. There was no alternative date; there were no leftovers to share. The forfeited seats were filled instead with those who were truly grateful to be invited. Those who attended were overjoyed; those who didn't missed the once-in-forever feast of the King.

For every choice that you make about what to do with your time, you make a decision not to do something else. Sometimes you may make these choices purposefully—leaving work early to make it to your child's school play. But other times you may be making these decisions and not even realize the consequences—watch a football game one afternoon and miss the chance to help your neighbors struggling with their car outside. This is not to say you shouldn't be allowed to relax every now and then. But we could all probably be a little more intentional with our schedules. Watch out for good you could be doing. And when you realize you've missed an opportunity, take steps not to let it happen again.

Don't overlook, or worse, reject, obvious invitations to join in the work of God's kingdom. God will invite you to the party, but he won't force you to attend.

It's Your Move!

An individual activity: For a few days keep a detailed journal of how you spend your discretionary time. Analyze the results. Contrast the amount of time spent on frivolous matters with time spent on genuine priorities. Where did your family rank in the analysis? How about God? What endeavor consumed the greatest amount of your time? Was it worth it?

A group activity: Together choose a spiritual priority and a strategy for accomplishing it. Here are a couple ideas to get the ball rolling:

- Priority: Christian service. Strategy: Organize and host a special program for a local nursing home—a volunteer concert, drama, Bible study, game night, etc.

- Priority: Christian discipline. Strategy: Develop a month-long prayer focus for your small group. For the next thirty days everyone will commit to praying daily for a specific need or request. Share together how that month of prayer impacted the need and/or the lives of those who prayed.

- Priority: Your choice. Strategy: Get creative!

BONUS

Make the Lord and your relationship with him the number one commitment of your life. Keep your priorities straight; anything less is just a trivial pursuit!

POINT

TABOO:
Acknowledging Temptation

PART ONE—GAME ON

Object of the Game

In this fast-paced word guessing game, sometimes all of the best and most useful words are off limits. It seems almost impossible to resist saying one of them. In a Christian's life, there are some things that are off limits as well. As you play through the game, think about the areas of your life where you find temptation hard to resist.

Game Preparation

Only one TABOO game set will be needed for this activity as it can be played by any group, no matter what the size. It is best to have all players seated in an open area where you can form a circle and each can participate easily. Have paper and pencil available for keeping score.

> "The trouble with trouble is that it usually starts out as a whole lot of fun."
> —Anonymous

If you like decorating for your small group meeting, try using the color red, a color often associated with temptation and sin. You could use red balloons or streamers, or just print out and hang up a lot of red "no entry" signs. If you do a Google search on "no entry signs," you can find many different ones available.

Though no one knows what the fruit of the forbidden tree in Eden actually was, for many people, a juicy red apple symbolizes temptation. So you could also add some color to your session with bowls of shiny red apples.

Playing by the Rules

Choose only two teams—how you pick the teams is up to you. If, for example, you are playing men against the women, alternate the team players around the circle—man, woman, man, etc. While one team is playing, the other team must have a player (the censor) watch to ensure the clue giver doesn't use any taboo words. If a taboo word is used, the censor sounds the buzzer. When play passes to the other team, the previous clue giver then becomes the censor. Game play continues until everyone has had a chance to be the clue giver.

To make the game a bit more challenging, have everyone in the circle turn their chairs to face outward. Guessing the right word is a little more difficult when the clue giver and team members are not so visible to each other.

For alternative play, try this. Have each team create a few cards for the opposition. These cards will feature Bible key words (proper names are allowed) along with biblical taboo clues. For example, if the key word was God, the taboo words might be Lord, Creator, Father, the Man Upstairs, etc.

TRIVIA

Brian Hersch, General Partner at Hersch and Company, is a real estate developer in partnership with his brother. Marketing land and houses is only one of the hats he wears. He is best known as the creator of such popular interactive games as TABOO, OUTBURST, and others. In 2003 he expanded his horizons yet again when he became executive producer for a television game show that was produced by and aired on The New TNN network. The forty episodes, hosted by comedian Chris Wylde, were based on his popular interactive game TABOO (sourced from http://www.prnewswire.com/cgi-bin/stories.pl?ACCT=105&STORY=/www/story/09-04-2002/0001794098, last viewed 6-3-09).

To Eat

Tempting contrasts should be the theme for snack time. Offer both rich, delectable snacks and healthy snacks side by side. Here are a few starter ideas.

- Prepare a platter of finger desserts: brownie squares, gooey butter cake squares, chocolate-chip cookies, etc. Place it next to a platter of raw vegetables: carrots, cucumber slices, celery, broccoli, or cauliflower pieces.

- Bake a pecan pie and serve it next to a bowl of mixed nuts.

- Serve a Colossal Carmel Apple Trifle (see recipe) alongside a large bowl of fresh fruit salad.

- Place a bowl of corn chips drizzled with Nacho cheese and fried ground beef next to a bowl of baked chips and salsa.

You get the idea. Be creative; see how many tempting foods you can pair with healthy alternatives. It will be interesting to see which food group has leftovers!

For Younger Players

Older children can play as part of the teams, but younger children might want to play a round of TABOO FOR KIDS. The words and action will be geared to their level of experience and understanding. Another idea would be to let the kids be the censors. They'll love hitting that buzzer and stopping the adults in their tracks.

If they are not interested in the game or if they can't read, have them draw a picture that shows how they imagine the Garden of Eden looked. Have them include the tree of the knowledge of good and evil and what, in their minds, the fruit was like. Follow up with a couple of questions:

- What does *temptation* mean? Give an example of a time when you were tempted.

- How do you resist temptation when it comes your way?

MIX IT UP

1 (18.25 OUNCE) PACKAGE
   YELLOW CAKE MIX

6 CUPS COLD MILK

3 (3.4 OUNCE) PACKAGES INSTANT
   VANILLA PUDDING MIX

1 TEASPOON APPLE PIE SPICE

1 (12 OUNCE) JAR CARAMEL ICE
   CREAM TOPPING

1 ½ CUPS CHOPPED PECANS,
   TOASTED

2 (21 OUNCE) CANS APPLE PIE
   FILLING

2 (16 OUNCE) CONTAINERS
   FROZEN WHIPPED
   TOPPING, THAWED

Prepare and bake the cake mix according to directions on the package. Use two greased, 9-inch round baking pans. Once finished baking, allow the cakes to cool completely. In a large bowl, whisk milk, pudding mixes, and apple pie spice for 2 minutes. Let stand for 2 minutes or until the mixture is soft-set.

Trim one cake layer, if necessary, so that it sits evenly in an 8-quart punch bowl (you can also use a trifle bowl, if you have one). Poke holes in the cake with a long wooden skewer. Then gradually pour a third of the caramel topping over the cake (you may want to slightly heat the caramel in the microwave so that it pours more easily). Sprinkle with ½ cup pecans and spread with half of the pudding mixture. Spoon one can of pie filling over pudding; spread with one carton of whipped topping.

Top with remaining cake and repeat layers. Then top it all off by drizzling the creation with remaining caramel topping and sprinkle with remaining pecans. Refrigerate until serving. (posted by Deborah Randall, http://allrecipes.com/Recipe/Colossal-Caramel-Apple-Trifle/Detail.aspx)

Picking Up the Pieces

As you are trying to recover from the sound of that buzzer, talk together about how life might be different if we all had such a buzzer with us every day—something that would alert us every time we were about to say or do the wrong thing.

All of us know what it's like to be tempted. All of us know what it's like to succumb to that temptation. You may see it differently, but after all these years of living, this is how I describe temptation: the lure of something forbidden and yet readily available.

Temptation is the challenge of getting away with something that we shouldn't. It is a battle we often lose because we don't put up much of a struggle. Temptation isn't logical. In a rational moment you can think of a thousand reasons why you shouldn't do what you are about to do, but unfortunately, moments of temptation are not rational. Our desires often override any sense of logic, or any inner buzzers that might be going off.

Temptation is the great equalizer—rich or poor, educated or uneducated, powerful or weak, young or old, male or female—not a soul escapes the powerful draw of temptation. Pray together to ask God for his:

- support to help us avoid temptation.

- hope to get us through our hardest struggles.

- mercy when we fail.

TAKE 🎲 TURNS

1. What do you think—are some people more easily tempted than others? Explain your answer.

2. What, in your estimation, is the biggest temptation facing Christians today, as a group?

TABOO:
Acknowledging Temptation

PART TWO—POSTGAME BREAKDOWN

Object of the Study

Sometimes God is unfairly thought of as a celestial killjoy who sadistically seeks to rob us of our fun. In actuality, God genuinely seeks to preserve our joy and sanity in life. His rules are for our protection. Let's examine some of the pitfalls of temptation, as well as principles that can help us rise above temptation's defeats. God is willing to help us if we are willing to humbly follow him. To experience a life of peace and freedom, we must remember that some things are just taboo.

Bible Content

> For a man's ways are in full view of the LORD,
> and he examines all his paths.
> The evil deeds of a wicked man ensnare him;
> the cords of his sin hold him fast.
> He will die for lack of discipline,
> led astray by his own great folly.
>
> —Proverbs 5:21-23

> This righteousness from God comes through faith in Jesus Christ to all who believe. There is no difference, for all have sinned and fall short of the glory of God, and are justified freely by his grace through the redemption that came by Christ Jesus.
>
> —Romans 3:22-24

> So, if you think you are standing firm, be careful that you don't fall! No temptation has seized you except what is common to man. And God is faithful; he will not let you be tempted beyond what you can bear. But when you are tempted, he will also provide a way out so that you can stand up under it.
>
> —1 Corinthians 10:12, 13

To Study

Explorer Captain James Cook is credited with adding islands to the world atlas, but did you know he also added words to the English dictionary? It's true. Taboo was a Polynesian word that Cook introduced to the English language from his travels around the world. In a journal entry from 1777, Cook says this word "has a very comprehensive meaning; but, in general, signifies that a thing is forbidden" (viewed on www.answers.com/topic/taboo on 6-4-09).

To list all taboos would be nearly impossible; hundreds of habits, behaviors, practices, issues, social faux pas, and cultural missteps would fill reams of paper. And yet all taboos share one thing in common—each represents temptation.

WHY AM I SO EASILY TEMPTED?

This question has probably passed through everyone's mind at one time or another. Let's look at three reasons temptation can be so hard to avoid.

We are imperfect. The apostle Paul writing in Romans 3:23 states it succinctly: "All have sinned and fall short of the glory of God." There is not a perfect person in your group—or any group! We have all met temptation face to face on the battlefield and lost. But remember, even perfect people encounter temptation. Jesus was tempted in every way just like we are. The difference? He never lost the battle and sinned.

TAKE TURNS

1. What are the major areas of temptation for most people? Are Christians any different from non-Christians when it comes to temptation?

2. How can we cope with our imperfection?

3. Do you believe in a literal devil or do you think Satan is just biblical imagery for evil deeds? Explain your answer.

1. What things, behaviors, or actions do you consider taboo in your life?

2. Where does your value system originate? Are your taboos based on your upbringing, your feelings, or your experiences? Or are they based on an outside source of authority?

A spiritual force of evil is at work. Consider these words from Ephesians 6:12: "For our struggle is not against flesh and blood, but against the rulers, against the authorities, against the powers of this dark world and against the spiritual forces of evil in the heavenly realms." Satan's desire is to ruin us physically, emotionally, mentally, and most of all spiritually. He leaves no stone unturned, no card unplayed, and no trick unused in his effort to bring us to defeat. He can bribe, coerce, induce, entice, compel, intimidate, threaten, frighten, and bully us. But he cannot make us yield against our wills. Ultimately, we have no one to blame for our sin but ourselves.

Good things can become a source of temptation. The word *taboo* can refer to something that is bad or evil, but in the culture from which the word originates, it was also used to refer to something that had been set apart as sacred. This sacred thing could not be touched by anyone (except possibly for their priests), or else harm would fall on that person from some supernatural force. So in such a case, it was not the thing itself that was bad, but it was the breaking of the tradition or cultural laws that brought on punishment.

Noah found grace in the eyes of the Lord. Following the flood, he celebrated a safe return to land—that was good. However, following the first harvest in the new world he celebrated too much and got drunk (Genesis 9). The fruit of God's creation is good, but when abused, it can lead to a life of defeat. Alcohol abuse can destroy your life or the lives of others.

Abraham, known as the friend of God, sought to protect his life and marriage—that was good. However, he did so at the cost of truth (Genesis 12). His dishonesty was exposed, his wife was disgraced, and his integrity was shattered. Honesty isn't an option for a Christian. It takes a lifetime to build a good reputation, but it can be destroyed overnight through deceit.

Moses was filled with a godly zeal for justice—that was good. However, his zeal at times exploded in anger. In a moment of indignant rage, Moses murdered an Egyptian taskmaster (Exodus 2). On another occasion his unchecked anger and disobedience also cost him entrance into the promised land. Anger can destroy your capacity to lead or serve God.

King David, a man after God's own heart, loved his wife—that was good. However, when he allowed that same God-created physical desire for intimacy to lead him into the arms of another man's wife, it nearly destroyed his life and home (2 Samuel 11). What began with a glance became a lingering look, which then exploded into a lustful longing. The whole disgusting story ended in an adulterous affair, an illegitimate pregnancy, a conspiracy to murder, and a nightmare for the entire nation of Israel. Struggling with uncontrolled sexual desires can destroy your marriage and your family.

TAKE TURNS

Try these activities to spark some discussion:

1. Temptation in a Hat—every person writes down a temptation on a slip of paper and drops it into a hat (or similar container). Mix the papers well and have each person draw a slip, read the temptation, and then suggest ways to resist or avoid the sin.

2. If You Could Take a Different Path—each person in the small group shares an experience where if life could be repeated, he or she would do it differently. What different path would you choose and why? How would your life be changed if you had taken that path the first time?

Fill in the blanks:

The thing that is a big temptation for me right now is _____

_____.

I could use these three strategies to deal with my temptation:

_____

_____

_____

Look at the verses from Proverbs 5 from the Bible Content section. "For a man's ways are in full view of the LORD, and he examines all his paths" (verse 21). Perhaps we need to have that verse posted on our mirrors, our doors, our computer monitors, our dashboards, our desks, and our cell phones. Would we be so quick to crumble under temptation if we remembered that God was watching our every move?

His rules truly are for our protection. God knows nothing will destroy your joy and sense of freedom more than being enslaved to your desires. Don't surrender to the counterfeit substitutes of God's love and grace. Fight hard—temptation is a formidable foe, but not unconquerable.

The counterfeits to God's blessings glitter with promise but bring pain instead: drug addiction, alcohol dependency, sexually transmitted diseases, pornographic obsession, indulgent eating, compulsive buying, irresponsible gambling, and on and on. We cling to the counterfeit when the genuine is not available. My friend Alan Philips described it like this, "We want warm, fresh-baked apple pie with ice cream, but we will settle for grape jelly on a cracker in its absence. So it is with the absence of genuine love—we'll settle for a cheap substitute."

Try these biblical and practical weapons when fighting against temptation.

Run when tempted. Isn't that cowardly? Not at all. Sometimes the wisest thing you can do is run away from temptation as fast as your feet will carry you. Someone offers you illegal drugs—run. Someone offers you a dishonest deal—walk away. The porn site pops up on the screen—hit delete and shut down the computer. Just run—and don't look back.

Fight when you can't run. Some temptations appear far more powerful than they are. Satan builds up impressive but empty decoys to mislead us. Take a closer look; things are not always what they seem to be. Examine the source of your temptation in God's sight. And try simply saying "No!" It's amazing how much power can be packed into that little word. James writes to encourage us in our resistance: "Submit yourselves, then, to God. Resist the devil, and he will flee from you" (James 4:7).

When possible, remove the temptation. Through exaggerated imagery Jesus makes the point that we need to remove the weakness that leads us into temptation's grip. "If your right eye causes you to sin, gouge it out and throw it away. It is better for you to lose one part of your body than for your whole body to be thrown into hell" (Matthew 5:29). You may not want to take your eye out, but you can avoid the places, persons, and things that feed into your weaknesses.

Find an accountability partner. Fighting temptation alone can be an overwhelming task, so ask someone you trust to hold you accountable in your weak areas. Perhaps you can do the same for that person. God created the church for just such a purpose—there is strength and support in numbers.

Trust God and pray. In those moments when we are in danger of crossing the line, we need to cling to God's promise: "No temptation has seized you except what is common to man. And God is faithful; he will not let you be tempted beyond what you can bear. But when you are tempted, he will also provide a way out so that you can stand up under it" (1 Corinthians 10:13).

It's Your Move!

If you are a parent, take inventory of what may create undue temptation in your home. Remove any inappropriate DVDs, magazines, music, or books that you own. If your child owns any such things, sit down and talk with him or her about why you think they are inappropriate. Try to lead your children into making wise choices on their own, rather than just throwing out their stuff with no warning. Take an interest in your child's friends. Do you know who they hang with? Is there a computer in your teen's room where you have no supervision of the programming being viewed? Keep the family computer in a place where everyone in the house can be held accountable. You can't keep your children from temptation but you can make it less available.

As a group, consider how you might help out support groups either at your church or in your community for people with addictions. If your church doesn't offer such a ministry, talk to the leadership about how you could get one started.

BONUS

The grace of God can overcome our greatest temptation. The mercy of God can cover our worst sin. The hope of God heals our past and points us to the future. The promise of God assures us of eternity.

POINT

OUTBURST:
Harnessing the Power of the Tongue

PART ONE—GAME ON

Object of the Game

Having a quick tongue can be an asset when playing the outspoken OUTBURST game. However, when your tongue is faster than your brain, watch out! That may spell trouble for other areas of life.

Game Preparation

Only one game set will be needed for this activity as the OUTBURST game can be played by any group size. It is best to have all players in an open area—players can stand or sit. Many people have a hard time sitting still in this game!

> "When the mouth stumbles, it is worse than the foot."
> —West African proverb

For this pre-game activity you will need a box of wooden tongue depressors. (Check your local medical supply store or family physician for this resource. Boxes usually contain one hundred depressors.) Divide your group into teams of three or four. Distribute the entire box equally among the teams. At the signal, each team has five minutes to pick a challenging word and spell it with the sticks. It must be legible to count. No dictionaries. The goal—to choose a word that will score the greatest number of points on the following scale:

- Longest word=1 point

- Most diverse use of letters=2 points

- Most sticks used=1 point

- Most vowels used=1 point

- If the other team doesn't know the definition=2 points

Give each member of the winning team a lollipop, popsicle, or some similar treat they can lick.

As was noted in the last game session, Brian Hersch, of Hersch and Company, was the creator of the OUTBURST game and the game of TABOO as well. Though the OUTBURST game has been discontinued by Hasbro, it's fairly easy to find a copy these days, considering during its time on the store shelves it generated 45 million units sold and over $850 million in retail sales. But if you or your neighbor doesn't already have a copy, you can check such distributors as eBay or Amazon.com—a recent search there produced more than ten versions of the game still available, including a junior edition, one for PCs, an anniversary edition, and the Bible edition.

Playing by the Rules

The OUTBURST game has hundreds of topics. Each game card contains ten target answers—there may be more right answers that are not included on the card, but only those on the card count toward accumulated points. Divide your group, regardless of its size, into two equal halves. How you determine the teams is up to you—you can draw straws, flip coins, or pick numbers; just make sure you end up with two reasonably equal teams.

Because the game can get a bit wild, you will need a trustworthy moderator. Choose one person from within the group who is both authoritative and honest. The moderator's role is to read the category for each team and keep track of correct answers. Given the fast-paced nature of the game, each team should provide a helper to assist the moderator when the opposing team is guessing. With so many people shouting out answers, it is hard for one person to listen and keep track of all that is being said.

If playing time is an issue, set a time limit for the game, set a turn limit, or reduce the number of points required for victory. For a different twist, add this rule: if a team guesses all answers on the card, the team keeps playing until an answer on subsequent cards is missed. Only then does the other team get a chance to play. If a team cannot guess any right answers on the card at all, ten points must be deducted from their score.

To make the game even more challenging (and quieter), appoint a team spokesperson for each round. Only the spokesperson can shout out the words. Other team members must whisper or write out their answers for the spokesperson to share. The spokesperson must change with every new card, which ensures everyone gets to participate in every aspect. (Listening and teamwork skills are needed for this variation.) Still too loud? Try a silent round. Only the moderator can speak to announce the topic and track the score. Team members are not allowed to talk among themselves but must write the answers on a dry-erase white board or a chalkboard. Hand signals between team members are allowed.

To Eat

"I scream, you scream, we all scream for ice cream!" Ice cream cones top the menu for this activity. Provide both wafer and sugar cones, along with a variety of ice cream flavors. For toppings, try bringing these: chocolate shell topping, fudge, fruit preserves, butterscotch and caramel sundae topping, chopped nuts, candy sprinkles, chocolate chips, and chopped up candies of various sorts. If preparation time is limited, your group could opt to use pre-packaged ice cream novelty items such as Drumsticks or Sundae Cones. You could also provide frozen yogurt and sorbet, just for something different.

Or, if ice cream sounds too chilly, try offering barbecue ribs, Buffalo chicken wings, or any other food that will give your group a chance to smack their lips and lick their fingers. One other main dish that comes to mind is not for the faint of heart. The connection should be obvious—tongue! It might be worth it to bring it to the session just to see the looks on people's faces when you tell them what you've brought for a snack.

Another fun eating activity might be an Oreo-licking contest. Both adults and children can participate in this one. Provide each contestant with a whole Oreo cookie. To win, a contestant must be the first person to take the cookie apart (without breaking either half) and lick the icing from both halves. At least two impartial judges will be needed for determining the winner. Good luck!

TAKE 🎲 TURNS

1. Go around the group and have each person share a time when he or she blurted out something that shouldn't have been said. What happened? Was it funny or just humiliating? How did you move on?

2. You've undoubtedly heard this expression: "Sticks and stones may break my bones, but words will never hurt me." Do you agree or disagree with that statement? Which heals faster—a physical injury or a verbal wound? Why?

For Younger Players

This is one of those games where the younger family members can easily participate with the adults on the team. If, however, the kids choose to play by themselves, a junior edition of the game is available. Kids who can read well can also serve as moderators or helpers. Or you could let the kids be the mouthpieces for your teams—everyone has to give answers to the kids on the teams. If an answer isn't shouted out by someone twelve and under, it doesn't count.

It might also be fun to include the kids in the Take Turns discussion for this session. You never know what you might learn from the mouths of babes!

Picking Up the Pieces

Once you catch your breath, take a moment to consider the power of the spoken word. Read Colossians 3:8-10. The tongue is the perpetrator of these sinful, undesirable qualities.

- How are they so damaging?

- What can you do to rid them from your life?

Read Proverbs 12:18 together: "Reckless words pierce like a sword, but the tongue of the wise brings healing." Use this as a basis for your closing prayer time. Pray that God will help you learn:

- the wisdom to know when to speak up and when to be silent.

- the will to control your tongue.

- the way to worship him with the words of your mouth.

OUTBURST:
Harnessing the Power of the Tongue

PART TWO—POSTGAME BREAKDOWN

Object of the Study

The OUTBURST game stands in contrast with the Spirit-filled life—there's nothing gentle, kind, loving, or peaceful about it. Unfortunately, our verbal interaction with others also often stands in contrast with the Spirit-filled life. For those moments, James supplies wisdom that can spare us a world of verbal hurt.

Bible Content

Everyone should be quick to listen, slow to speak and slow to become angry, for man's anger does not bring about the righteous life that God desires. Therefore, get rid of all moral filth and the evil that is so prevalent and humbly accept the word planted in you, which can save you.

—James 1:19-21

When we put bits into the mouths of horses to make them obey us, we can turn the whole animal. Or take ships as an example. Although they are so large and are driven by strong winds, they are steered by a very small rudder wherever the pilot wants to go. Likewise the tongue is a small part of the body, but it makes great boasts. Consider what a great forest is set on fire by a small spark. The tongue also is a fire, a world of evil among the parts of the body. It corrupts the whole person, sets the whole course of his life on fire, and is itself set on fire by hell.

All kinds of animals, birds, reptiles and creatures of the sea are being tamed and have been tamed by man, but no man can tame the tongue. It is a restless evil, full of deadly poison. With the tongue we praise our Lord and Father, and with it we curse men, who have been made in God's likeness. Out of the same mouth come praise and cursing. My brothers, this should not be. Can both fresh water and salt water flow from the same spring? My brothers, can a fig tree bear olives, or a grapevine bear figs? Neither can a salt spring produce fresh water.

—James 3:3-12

To Study

If you like practicality then the letter James wrote ought to be on your list of favorite reads. James doesn't write in the lofty altitudes of philosophical conjecture, he brings the issues down to ground level where we live. That may explain why he spends more time addressing the work of the tongue than any other epistle. His counsel is both wise and practical. Consider these truths.

TAKE YOUR TIME BEFORE YOU SPEAK

Do you ever start your mouth before putting your brain in gear? Welcome to the crowd. There is no quick and easy cure for foot-in-mouth disease. Who among us hasn't known the unpleasant taste of shoe leather?

TAKE TURNS

1. What tongue trippers are most problematic for people in the church? Why?

2. What's one tongue problem you used to have when you were younger that you have learned to control? How did you manage it? Share your successes with the group.

3. Our mothers used to tell us: "If you can't say something nice, don't say anything at all." Do you think this statement still holds true for adult life? Why or why not?

1. What tongue trippers are most problematic for you person-ally? Why?

2. How can you improve your ability to listen:
   - to God?
   - to those you love?
   - to your critics?

James warns us how dangerous the tongue can be:

- The tongue contributes to our inability to listen (1:19)—one tongue works harder but less efficiently than two ears.

- The tongue contributes to our hypocrisy (3:9-12)—the tongue, more than any other part of us, betrays our hypocritical nature. How can we lift our voices to God with such words as, "O for a thousand tongues to sing my great Redeemer's praise," and then turn around and with those same tongues curse the life he has so graciously provided? We can be so incon-sistent. Fresh water and salt water don't flow from the same spring, but too often refreshing thoughts and salty language do flow from the same tongue. Hypocrisy!

- The tongue contributes to our desire to gossip (3:6)—I fear that the church has made gossip the Christian's acceptable sin. We know we can't believe everything we hear, but no one ever said we couldn't repeat it. And have you noticed that gossip always seems to travel faster over grapevines that are slightly sour? Gossip is like mud thrown on a clean wall. It may not stick, but it always leaves a dirty mark. It's a fire we Christians seem reluctant to extinguish.

Does James recommend any way to avoid these dangers? Certainly.

- Listen more; talk less. Our communication skills will never progress beyond the most rudimentary levels if we don't learn to listen better.

1. What things trigger your angry tongue?

2. Think of at least three times in the past week that you said something in anger or haste. Jot them down.

3. Looking back, what could you have done to have avoided letting your tongue take control of you?

- Listen to God: everything we need for developing spiritual maturity is contained in the Bible. God's Word provides advice on attitudes, marriage, parenting, working relationships, friendship, worship, money management, leisure, materialism, benevolence, and much more.

- Listen to those you love: trusted friends and family have your best interest at heart, so pay close attention to their helpful advice.

- Listen to your critics: as painful as criticism may be, there is something to be learned from it. Even those whose company we may not enjoy can speak wisely, if we will listen. "As iron sharpens iron, so one man sharpens another" (Proverbs 27:17).

Take your time. Be quick to listen and slow to speak.

TAKE CONTROL, BEFORE YOU BECOME ANGRY

We dare not leave out the last third of verse 19, "Everyone should be quick to listen, slow to speak and slow to become angry."

Anger can be displayed in many ways, but the most common expression of anger is our speech. Harsh words, vulgar expressions, painful name-calling, filthy humor—not quite what one would expect from a Christian, and yet we've all stumbled with our tongues. We speak in the passion of the moment, then later regret our choice of words. When our thoughtless outbursts lead to angry outbursts we're in deep trouble. Don't lose heart; James has more insights to share.

James warns that the tongue is a fire. Good analogy. A controlled fire is a useful and power tool, but once out of control, a raging fire is devastating.

- Fire creates heat. When angered we engage in heated arguments and fiery language.

- Fire destroys. I will never forget the sights, sounds, and smells of the fire that destroyed the Sherwood Oaks Christian Church building in the fall of 1991. To this day the rescued items from my office still retain the acrid odor of that black, billowing smoke. In similar fashion, I've seen fiery words destroy careers, marriages, parent/child relationships, friendships, self-esteem, confidence, hope, and the desire to keep on living. And that's just the short list.

- Fire leaves scars. Anyone who has ever endured serious burns must live with the visible, sometimes hideous scars. We too easily forget that words spoken in heated arguments also leave scars long after the passion and emotion has cooled.

- James reminds his readers that the source of the tongue's fiery nature is hell itself (verse 6). The word is *Gehenna*, the name of the refuse dump outside the city of Jerusalem where the fires burned continually. What a fitting description for the smoldering garbage that often tumbles from the tongue.

Again, does James offer a way to put out the fire of the tongue? Yes, but it isn't an easy fix. James offers only one solution—control it! To illustrate, James points us to three controlling objects: a bit in a horse's mouth, a rudder on a ship, and a spark that ignites a forest fire. In relation to what is being controlled, the object of control is much smaller. Such is the power of the tongue. I read this warning label on a fountain pen some years ago: "When this pen runs too freely, it is nearly empty." Let's adapt that label for this lesson: "When this tongue runs too freely, the brain is nearly empty." Nothing indicates a weak mind more than an overly active tongue. God intended for our

"The tongue is the only instrument that grows sharper with use."
—Anonymous

minds to control our mouths; unfortunately, most of us are guilty of the reverse. Take control, before you start a fire.

TAKE TURNS

1. How can the words of the tongue fuel the fire of anger?

2. In what way can listening act as a fire extinguisher?

3. How can you repair scars that you have inflicted on others with your tongue? What can you do to repair the damage of an uncontrolled tongue?

It's Your Move!

As an exercise in the positive use of one's tongue, go around the circle clockwise and say something positive about the person on your left. Once around the circle, reverse the direction and say something positive about the person on your right. Positive encouragement goes a long way in overcoming the negative power of the tongue. Being positive requires practice. The tongue's default mode is negativity.

Identify some folks you know personally who have been on the receiving end of a tongue lashing, an angry outburst, or the subject of some sordid gossip barrage. In a quiet, thoughtful way, determine what you can do to encourage those folks with your words and actions—a phone call, a brief visit, or a greeting card with one of those recordable messages. Send a note expressing your appreciation for the positive qualities in that person's character. Create a CD with positive thoughts, pictures, and quotes. Mail it anonymously.

Encourage the leadership of your church to offer a class on ways to avoid gossip. Your small group could sponsor the class and provide the materials. Study books on the subject are available.

BONUS

Let what you say
and how you say it
be a reflection of the
Lord, who was always
self-controlled.

POINT

ABOUT THE AUTHOR

Tom Ellsworth has served as the preaching minister at Sherwood Oaks Christian Church in Bloomington, Indiana, since 1981. It was there that he delivered the sermon series that became the seed of inspiration for this book. Tom is grateful for the friendship, spiritual insight, and encouraging leadership of his peers in ministry Jeff Faull, Gary Johnson, Sean Olson, and Billy Strother, who all worked together with him to develop "The Games People Play" sermon series.

In his free time, he enjoys aviation history and tinkering with his 1948 Chrysler. Mostly he loves spending time with his wife, Elsie, and their two grown daughters, together with their families. Tom is also the author of the Standard Publishing resources *It's Your Move—On Board* and *Beyond Your Backyard* (with *Beyond Your Backyard Group Member Discussion Guide*), and co-authored *Preaching James* (Chalice Press).